**Lewd, crude and**

She offe
he hone
Throughout the night
he did all right –
he was constantly on 'er and off 'er
– *Mike Beal, 69, Plymouth*

There was once a young nun called Vera
who wouldn't let anyone near her,
when a crafty old monk
jumped into her bunk
and now she is a Mother Superior.
– *Jean, 70, County Down, Northern Ireland*

## ABOUT THE COMPILER

Michael Rosen has been described as the 'poet laureate of post-war youth'. He has over a hundred books for children to his name, nearly all of which are a wicked mix of rumbustious humour, word-play and sharp observation. He is a regular contributor to radio and TV, hosting BBC Radio 4's *Treasure Islands* and BBC World Service's *Meridian Books*. His research into children's literature and children's own writing takes him all over the world – to the USA, Canada, Australia – and in the last twenty years he has visited over a thousand schools performing his own work. He has written several books for adults including *Goodies and Daddies*, a lighthearted guide to fatherhood, and has recently edited *The Penguin Book of Childhood*. He is currently researching the changing portrayal of childhood in children's literature.

*Rude Rhymes* is also published by Signet.

# RUDE RHYMES 2

## 2

The Bastard Child of
**RUDE RHYMES**

**COLLECTED BY MICHAEL ROSEN**
**ILLUSTRATED BY RIANA DUNCAN**

A SIGNET BOOK

SIGNET

Published by the Penguin Group
Penguin Books Ltd, 27 Wrights Lane, London w8 5TZ, England
Penguin Books USA Inc., 375 Hudson Street, New York, New York 10014, USA
Penguin Books Australia Ltd, Ringwood, Victoria, Australia
Penguin Books Canada Ltd, 10 Alcorn Avenue, Toronto, Ontario, Canada M4V 3B2
Penguin Books (NZ) Ltd, 182–190 Wairau Road, Auckland 10, New Zealand

Penguin Books Ltd, Registered Offices: Harmondsworth, Middlesex, England

First published 1994
1 3 5 7 9 10 8 6 4 2

Collection copyright © Michael Rosen, 1994
Illustrations copyright © Riana Duncan, 1994
All rights reserved

The moral right of the editor has been asserted

Filmset by Datix International Limited, Bungay, Suffolk
Printed in England by Clays Ltd, St Ives plc
Set in 10/12.5 pt Monophoto Plantin

# Contents

# Introduction

In *Rude Rhymes* (published in 1992) I asked for more songs, rhymes, riddles, definitions, puns, one-liners or any other rudeness. And lo! Hundreds of people replied. So here is a selection from their letters along with the fruits of my usual burrowings around in the world of oral vulgarity.

Now you may think that all you have in your hand, as you read this, is just another little collection of filth. And you'd be right. But you will also be thrilled to know that the two volumes combined represent the biggest and best collection of vulgar folklore available to the general public. Far be it from me to suggest that biggest is always best, but I think in this case this is so. Historians and sociologists in years to come will ponder on the people's state of mind in the 1990s, and they will be able to turn to the two *Rude Rhymes* collections and see a part of the popular imagination usually hidden from view.

In fact, this book is one long saga on the subject of 'hidden from view'. Recent events in the lives and loves of public figures throw an interesting light on how the British view this subject: with fascination and shame. If you're fascinated, you should be ashamed; and, more significantly, if you're ashamed, you're probably fascinated. People much cleverer than me have written how a significant part of our history can be told as a history of how we describe and think of our bodies. Just one glimpse: why, as late as the 1920s, was the English medical profession binding little children's legs in splints if their parents caught them playing with themselves? (See *The Penguin Book of Childhood*.) What were they all afraid of?

On another note, collecting folklore like this can

turn you into someone who sees words in a one-track way. One letter came signed by P. Niss, which I assumed was a joke but it soon had me looking at everyone else's name and address very closely. What of Sarah Pett-Noble? I thought maybe it was an order – Sarah, pet Noble! Someone wrote from Gladys Avenue ... oho, 'avin' you, is she? The landlady of the Travellers' Rest Inn who sent me some stuff reminded me of the landlady who kept the Cock Inn. I suppose it's just that travellers take it easy. The woman from Quickley Lane must be a bit breathless and the man from Thingwall must have interesting wallpaper. Someone boastful came from Dunmore. There was a Justin, which I've always thought was better than just out. Mr Pulling didn't tell me what he was pulling, and I suppose if you live in Rutland anything can happen. Mrs Longson should be very proud of her lad, while Claire Wilcock is probably best left to her own devices.

Once again, it was nice to get letters smelling of innocence: you will notice that one Angelina was a helpful contributor. Someone wrote from a house called Paradise, and many thanks to Dora Darling. My own name was constantly turned and twisted when I was a boy. After my friends and enemies turned Rosen to Rosie, all that remained was to figure out what exactly it was that could be rosy. They ended up with Rosiebum. But they never saw it ... how did they know?

It's just possible that there are yet more rhymes, ditties, puns, book titles, graffiti, etc., that I haven't collected in these two books. If so, rush them to Michael Rosen, c/o Signet Books, 27 Wrights Lane, London W8 5TZ.

## Bionic Fred

This is the tale of your Freddie Law
whose sexual equipment got jammed in the door.
By the time they freed him, he didn't feel well
for his private parts were mangled to hell.

They rushed him to hospital, the ambulance flew,
but when they arrived, there's nowt they could do.
What a bad blow for Fred, condemned without
    choice,
to live with no sex and a high squeaking voice.

But lucky for Fred, so he wouldn't feel a fool,
some bright spark suggested a 'Bionic Tool'.
A smart new electric one, made out of brass,
though the batteries would have to be kept up his
    arse.

Now newly equipped and after a rest,
Fred thought he would put the tool to the test.
So finding a woman, the nearest one handy,
supplied her with drink and made her feel randy.

She, without waiting, put her hand in Fred's flies,
as she felt what was there, gave a cry of surprise.
'That's my Bionic Chopper. Now let's have some
    fun.'
'Cor blimey,' she said, 'it felt like a gun.'

They both stripped quick and Fred entered her fast,
he turned up the control knob and gave her full blast.
They clung to each other as Fred's dick shook some
    more,
then they bounced off the bed and on to the floor.

Now the pace hotted up and they started to choke,
as the room became filled with dirty blue smoke.
With a bang Fred's left bollock shot up in the air
and his other one went bonketty-bonk down the stair.

So back for repair went Fred, full of woe.
Was this how his sex life was destined to go?
To return to his doctor at the end of each shag
with his tool in his pocket and his balls in a bag?

But they fixed up young Fred, made him manly again,
for they boosted his batteries with a flex from the
    main.
So if he can't get a girl, now poor Fred doesn't cry, –
he just flicks the switch and jerks himself dry.

Alexandra McCole, 24
Rochdale, Lancashire

In days of old,
when knights were bold,
and women weren't invented,
men rubbed their cocks
between two rocks
and went away contented.

Paul Davis
NSW, Australia


She offered her honour,
he honoured her offer.
Throughout the night
he did all right –
he was constantly on 'er and off 'er.

Mike Beal, 69
Plymouth, Devon

What's the time?
Half past nine.
Hang your knickers
on the line.

When the teacher
rings the bell,
pull her tits
and run like hell.

Hold on
what's that light?
Holy shit!
It's dynamite.

With a nick-nack
paddywhack
give a dog a bone.
School blows up
and we go home.

Nick the Dick, 13
Newport, Gwent


There's a place in France
where the naked ladies dance.
There's a hole in the wall
where the men see it all.
The kids don't care
'cos they nicked the underwear . . .

Boy, 9
Congleton, Cheshire

When God was giving out good looks,
there was a big long queue.
I was somewhere near the top.
Where the fuck was you?

Bernadette Kellett, 21
County Monaghan, Ireland


I wish I was a bar of soap
floating in your hand,
and every time you took a bath,
I'd see your Promised Land.

Bernadette Kellett, 21
County Monaghan, Ireland

Julius Caesar,
the Roman geezer,
squashed his nuts
in a lemon squeezer.

Jodie, 14
Plymouth, Devon

How do I know that my youth is all spent?
Well, my get-up-and-go has got up and went.
But I really don't mind when I think with a grin
of all the grand places my get-up has bin.

Jodie, 14
Plymouth, Devon

I'll tell you a story that's certain to please
of a great farting contest at Shitton-on-Pees,
where all the great arseholes parade in a field
to compete for a cup and for various shields.

Now old Mrs Potluck thought nothing of this:
she'd had some weak tea and was all wind and piss.
With her hands on her hips and her legs open wide
she unfortunately shit – and was disqualified.

Malcolm Hutchings, 55
Walton-on-the-Naze, Essex

Mummy, I saw the window-cleaner,
the nurse and the dustman having it away.
Mummy, I saw them all doing it,
just the other day.

The window-cleaner had his overalls on
with a shammy in his hand,
and the nurse had a stethoscope
in a place not too grand.

The couch it was a-shaking
and the dustman wasn't too pleased
when a certain part of his body
got accidentally squeezed.

So, Mummy, tell me all about it,
tell me why you were there,
prancing around happily
in your black underwear.

Khristina Rainford
Liverpool

My Aunty Mary
bragged about being hairy,
though everyone called her a liar.

My Uncle Bob lighted a match
and caused a big bush fire.

Khristina Rainford
Liverpool

I've had Liverpool's football team
and I've had you all.
I've had women by their privates
and fellas by their balls.
I told Old John down the street,
'One day I'm gonna catch yer
'cos I love to play at being sincere and sweet
and my name's Margaret Thatcher.'

Khristina Rainford
Liverpool

There was a young girl called Sarah
who liked to go horse-riding at Windsor
she went there one day
and to her dismay
saw a man having a pee up a tree.

Now Henry her horse was very hungry
and liked carrots and that sort of thing,
so when you go riding at Windsor
look out for a grave by a tree,
for there lies the remains of the dick
of the man who pissed up the tree.

Keith, 26
London

This is the tale of Daniel Morgan
who had a tiny sexual organ.
This gave the girls a sudden shock
when they held his tiny cock.

He laboured hard to find a cure
and poulticed it with fish manure.
He tied it up with bits of string,
but still it was a poor wee thing.

It was one inch long when fully reared
and, lying down, it disappeared.
'Twas just by chance they'd called him Danny –
with half-inch less, they'd've called him Fanny.

One day Dan read in the *Daily Mail*
that things called falsies were on sale
for women who had tiny breasts:
they wore these things inside their vests

And then went out in latest fashion
to satisfy men's beastly passions.
Our Danny said, 'I'm no fool.
I'll make myself a big false tool.'

He worked all night upon his chopper,
and ended up with a great big whopper.
Twelve inches long and made of plastic,
to stretch a fanny like elastic.

It was, when he'd finished, a lovely job:
upon the end, a big red knob.
Dan tied it on with bits of twine,
it really did look rather fine.

Lying there beneath his pants
it looked just like an elephant's.
Girls soon flocked all around with glee,
to see the bulge stretch to his knee.

No other fellas stood a chance
when Dan was at the local dance.
When girls were dancing round with Danny
his tool kept tickling round their fanny.

The girls began to faint and swoon
as Danny whisked them round the room.
But what a shock Dan had in store,
for one night dancing round the floor . . .

. . . Danny stopped and loudly cursed
as he felt his strings and strappings burst.
Before he'd reached the nearest seat,
his tool was dangling at his feet.

His partner said with a nervous cough,
'Excuse me, but your cock's fell off.'
He couldn't face the scene thereafter –
the wisecracks and the scornful laughter,

all these girls that Danny had dated
in tears to see his cock deflated.
A girl named Sylvia made him sick,
as she gave his tool a spiteful kick.

Poor Danny screamed around the hall
for the string was still tied around one ball.
And as he staggered to the door,
he dragged his cock along the floor.

The band by now were almost crackers
as Dan went off to bathe his knackers.
So if you are like Daniel Morgan
and have a tiny sexual organ . . .

. . . Remember, though it's only wee,
it's always good enough to pee.

Angela Ward, 30
Doncaster, South Yorkshire

Tiny Tim was very dim:
when he was taught to swim,
instead of floating on his tummy
picked his nose
and sucked his bummy.

Little Andy stole some candy,
said it would come in handy
to trip old ladies in the street
with the brightly coloured sweet.
Only a policeman overheard what he said
now little Andy's in home in bed with PC's Fred.

Little Billy and Little Willy
did some things extremely silly.

Little Mary's bum was hairy
so she wiped it clean with her mum's canary.

There was a lad whose name was Pete
who hated anything that tasted sweet.
He dipped a biscuit in his drink
and yelled, 'Oh, shit! What's that stink?'
'I'm not surprised,' his mother said,
'that biscuit's been under your bed.'
'Oh, that one,' added brother Mick
'that was where the dog was sick.'

Little Gus sat on the bus
fidgeting around in his seat
when his mother told him off
he pulled out his cock
and sucked on its teat.

When Uncle James joined the Navy,
he took on deck a pot of gravy.
When Captain Cloggs asked, 'What is that?'
James pulled down his pants and stuck out his twat.

Sean Slobber had a mouse
that gave his mummy such a fit.
The little mouse ran out the house
and ended up as cat shit.

Naomi from London
Accrington, Lancashire

I found she had two arseholes
which gave me quite a start,
for I've never in my life before
heard a stereophonic fart.

'Bob Smartass', 23
Oxford

Julius Caesar
let a breezer
in the English Channel.
The Channel stunk,
the warship sunk,
and Julius Caesar drowned.

Man, 62
Victoria, Australia


Here comes Doctor Ormister,
sliding down the banister.
Are you better? Are you worse?
Oh, good gracious, where's that nurse?

Here comes the nurse with a red-hot poultice,
puts it on and takes no notice.
'Ow!' said the patient, 'that's too hot.'
'Oh! said the nurse, 'I'm sure it's not.'

Here comes Doctor with a six-inch pin,
pulls it out and sticks it in.
'Oh!' said the patient, 'Stop!' said the nurse,
'If you do that you will make it worse.'

Woman, 35
Hampshire

Slimy Sam took his wife
to see the engine shunt.
The engine shunted backwards
and hit her up the

Country horses are the best
for carrying the coal.
The coal they cannot carry
they shove it up their

Holy Moses
had a son called Hence
who climbed a fence
and fell on his

Bollock and Bill
went up the hill
to have a game of cricket.
The ball went up his trouser leg
and hit his middle wicket.

Jodie Brett, 13
Peterborough, Cambridgeshire

Me not silly,
me not dumb,
me hold on to daddy's bum.
It go boom!
I go zoom!
That's how I get here so soon.

Sarah Anderson, 10
Leighton Buzzard, Bedfordshire


The boy stood on the burning deck,
eating red-hot scallops.
He dropped one down his trouser leg
and burnt off both his bollocks.

Boy, 10
London

Geoffrey and Bungle
are in the jungle:
Geoffrey's fucking in the grass.
Then along came Zippy,
the mighty hippy,
with an arrow up his arse.

Miss Thornton, 14
Chipping Norton, Oxfordshire


Roses are red
my balls are too,
but they're turning blue
from fucking you.

Jayne Nash, 12
Avebury, Wiltshire

I was walking down the lane
swinging my chain
when I bumped into a copper
and he took my name.
I pulled out my penknife,
flicketty flick,
chopped two quarters
off his dick.
Hospital he had to go –
balls an' all he had to show.
Two months later,
in a county jail,
I was scratching my balls
on a rusty nail.

M. Mullins, 12
London

I have a little problem
and many it appals:
I love the smell of semen
and I can't stop groping balls.

Most men they enjoy it
and some think I'm a tease,
but, though I try, I can't resist
temptation of a squeeze.

The ones that make me laugh
are those that hang down low.
I caress them and I tickle
as they dangle to and fro.

My favourites are the plump ones,
so if any of you men
have big fat hairy goolies,
can I stroke and fondle them?

Susie
Maidenhead, Berkshire

In the parlour, there were three:
you, the parlour light and me.
Three's a crowd, there is no doubt,
so the parlour light went out.

Claire Wilcock, 18
Nelson, Lancashire


Dogs do it, cats do it,
monkeys have a try.
Mums do it, dads do it,
so why don't you and I?

Claire Wilcock, 18
Nelson, Lancashire

My knickers are blue,
my knickers are brown,
but when I'm with you
my knickers are down.

Claire Wilcock, 18
Nelson, Lancashire


In Brighton she was Bridget.
She was Patsy up in Perth.
In Cambridge she was Clarissa,
the grandest girl on earth.
In Stafford she was Stella,
the best of all the bunch,
but down on his expense account
she was petrol, oil and lunch.

Claire Wilcock, 18
Nelson, Lancashire

Little Tommy with a grin
drank up all his daddy's gin.
Mummy said, when he was plastered,
'Go to bed you little . . . darling.'

Claire Wilcock, 18
Nelson, Lancashire


Mud is mud,
muck is muck,
but what's a kiss
without a fuck?

Lorraine Whyte, 22
County Antrim, Northern Ireland


He wore a daffodil, she wore a rose;
they both were arrested for wearing no clothes.

Lorraine Whyte, 22
County Antrim, Northern Ireland

Up in the loft where the lamplight flickers,
you lost your heart, and I lost my knickers.

Lorraine Whyte, 22
County Antrim, Northern Ireland


Ashes to ashes, dust to dust:
if you don't like my jumper
get your hands off my bust,

Lorraine Whyte, 22
County Antrim, Northern Ireland


Put your wee thing to my wee thing
till your wee thing goes red.
Don't be mistaken, don't be misled –
it's only me lighting my fag.

Lorraine Whyte, 22
County Antrim, Northern Ireland

If I were in a wood
And I were in the mood,
I would.
Would you?

Lorraine Whyte, 22
County Antrim, Northern Ireland


Janet and John
to a dance have gone –
they left half an hour ago.
They hadn't gone far
when John stopped the car
and said, 'For a widdle, I must go.
I will go for a pee
up yonder tree
I shall only be a moment or so.'
Janet said, 'Coo,
I'll come too,'
and wrote his name in the snow.

Man, 52
Radcliffe-on-Trent, Nottingham

Love it is a funny thing;
it makes of man a fool.
It takes away his appetite
and wears away his tool.

Man, 52
Radcliffe-on-Trent, Nottingham


He grabbed me round my slender neck –
I could not shout or scream.
He carried me into his room
where we would not be seen.
He tore away my flimsy wrap
and gazed upon my form –
I was so cold and still and damp,
while he was wet and warm.
His feverish mouth he pressed to mine –
I let him have his way –
he drained me of my very self,
I could not say him nay.
He made me what I am – alas!
That's why you find me here . . .
a broken vessel – broken glass –
that once held bottled beer.

Sarah Mason
Clwyd, Wales

## A Smoker's Ditty

Little Willy Woodbine
took Mary Goldflake
down Park Drive.
Took her behind the Capstan,
laid her upon the Turf,
took out his Thick Twist
and gave her a Light Shag.

Dave Harrison, 57
Saltash, Cornwall

*As in Toshiba advert*

## Our Warehouse Manager

Mick's the man who don't like work
he likes to sit on his bum and shirk.
He hides himself in his office
and plays with his thingummybob.
It's a tickly sort of job
getting work out of Mickamabob.
The lazy bugger only wants to snore
wants to snore
So don't come in his office too quick
you'll only find him holding his dick
and nervous girls will start to shout and roar.

Mrs X, 37
London


She stood on the bridge at midnight:
her lips were all a-quiver.
She gave a cough,
her tits dropped off
and went floating in the river.

Sarah, 16
Leeds, Yorkshire

Uncle George and Auntie Mabel
fainted at the breakfast table.
Children, let this be your warning:
never do it in the morning.

Phospherina's put them right.
now they do it morn and night.
Uncle George is hoping soon
to do it in the afternoon.

Uncle George is much improved,
since he's had them both removed.
Now he's free from base desire,
sits at home and pokes the fire.

Dave Johnstone, 44
Crowborough, East Sussex.

Don't let your dingle dangle in the dirt –
put it in your pocket where it won't get hurt.
If you haven't got a pocket, put it in your shirt,
but don't let your dingle dangle in the dirt.

Leanne Shepherd, 20
NSW, Australia

There was an old man
who, when asleep,
went on the rampage
and shagged loads of sheep.
He'd wake feeling dull
and rattle his skull
thinking, why is my willy all covered in wool?

Andy Hayes, 15
Amersham, Buckinghamshire

I went out with my boyfriend
to buy some bubblegum,
and when he wasn't looking
I stuck it up his bum.

Girl, 9
Swindon, Wiltshire

Love is fun, sex is a game,
boys do all the fucking, girls get all the blame.
One night's pleasure for nine months' pain,
baby in the hospital without a fucking name.
Boys are bastards, they call a girl a whore,
and none of this would've happened if Johnny hadn't
    tore.

Nicola Colohan, 18
County Sligo, Eire


Hairy Mary she got drunk,
she fell into a sailor's bunk,
and all the sailors had a dunk
in Hairy Mary's hairy cunt.

Jean, 70
County Down, Northern Ireland

It's a hell of a life,
said the Queen of Spain,
ten minutes' pleasure
and nine months' pain,
three months' holiday
and we start again.
It's a hell of a life,
said the Queen of Spain.

Mrs H. Preedy
Kingston-upon-Thames, Surrey

37

Whatever mother said to you,
it isn't just for pissing through.
You should use it when you can
to please yourself and please your man.

CLH (girl), 14
Dolgellau, Wales


I'm a very good girl
I don't swear.
Shit, bugger, arsehole,
I don't care.

CLH (girl), 14
Dolgellau, Wales

## The Robin

A little robin perched upon my window sill
to hail the coming morn,
and brought the joy and gaiety
when all sweet things are born.

He was so small and fragile
but sweetly did he sing,
so there into my heart
thoughts of happiness did spring.

I smiled gently at his song
and paused beside my bed
then gently closed the window
and smashed his fucking head.

Angelina Curzey, 17
Birmingham

My days of youth are over,
my torch of life burned out;
what used to be my sex appeal
is now my water spout.

Time was when of its own accord
'twould from my trousers spring,
but now I have a full-time job
to find the fucking thing.

It used to be amusing,
the way it would behave
when in the early morning
it stood and watched me shave.

As my old age approaches
it now gives me the blues
to see it hang its withered head
and watch me clean my shoes.

Man, 52
Bolton, Lancashire

The snowman in my garden said,
'You humans must be thick.
You made me eyes, a nose and mouth,
but where the hell's my dick?'

Mrs Wendy Evans, 30
Whitchurch, Shropshire

From the kitchen swiftly came
a smell that was delicious.
But the turkey in the microwave
began to get suspicious . . .
'I wonder why I feel so hot
and why have I been plucked?
Then suddenly it dawned on him
'Oh, dear, I think I'm fucked!'

Mrs Wendy Evans, 30
Whitchurch, Shropshire


Rabbits build warrens,
birds build a nest.
Come over here
and I'll show you my breast.

Bowls made of glass,
cups made of china.
Pull down my panties
and stroke my vagina.

Woman
Hertfordshire

Josie had a dream
A dream that made her laugh.
She dreamt she was a bar of soap
whilst Ricky was in the bath.

Josie had another dream
which gave her a little shock.
She dreamt Ricky was in her bed,
with his cock stuck up her frock.

Josie had a dream
a dream that made her giggle.
She dreamt that Ricky was still in her bed
and gave a mighty wiggle.

Josie had another dream
a dream that broke her heart.
She dreamt Ricky was still inside her
And gave a little fart.

Josie had a dream
A dream that made her cry.
She asked Ricky to do it again
And he wouldn't even try.

Katherine, 14
Southend, Essex.

Oh, dark and slimy slit,
how we all long for it,
separated from the arsehole
by a little tiny bit.
Hold on, you little tiny bit,
or we'll all be in the shit.

D. J. Rodgers
Farnborough, Hampshire

## The Cuckoo

A strange bird is the cuckoo:
it sits upon the grass.
Its wings are neatly folded,
its beak stuck up its arse.
And from this strange position
It sings its song, 'Twit, twit' . . .

. . . well, you try singing, 'Cuckoo'
with a beak full of shit!

D. J. Rodgers
Farnborough, Hampshire

'Father, oh, Father, I've come to confess
I've left a poor girl in a hell of a mess.
Her knickers all tattered, her tits are all bare,
and there is something inside her that shouldn't be
    there.'

'Son, oh, son, you should have known better
in my young days we used a French letter.'
'Father, oh, Father, you do me unjust,
I used a French letter, but the fucking thing bust.'

D. J. Rodgers
Farnborough, Hampshire

45

One very hot day, in the summer last year,
a young man was swimming around Brighton Pier.
He dived underneath and he swam to a rock,
and amused all the young ladies by shaking his . . . fist
at a policeman who stood on the shore,
the very same copper who copped him before.
For the copper to order him out for a farce,
the cheeky young man just showed him his . . . clever
    manoeuvres and wonderful pace
and when he got cross, he just laughed in his face.
Now this lad had a lassie and they would go for a swim
and he would swim all the way with his hand on her
    . . . chest
to support her, should she get tired,
a kindly attention this young girl admired.
He swam like an otter, she swam like a duck
and they would end the morning by having a . . . nice
    bit of lunch and a bottle of wine,
a treat which few ladies would ever decline.
They stroll around the beach and she starts to hunt
for pieces of seaweed to hang round her . . . bedroom
    windows a reminder to be,
of the happy days they'd spent by the sea.
Now, if for a moment his lady he'd miss,
he'd wager his life, she was doing a . . . a kind
    thoughtful action by kiss or caress,
by soothing kiddies who were in distress.

The day is now ended and evening tide falls,
she would amuse her young man by tickling his . . .
     fancy with tales of life
she will be to him his dear little wife.
The darkness surrounds them so closely they lay,
which is which of them is awkward to say.
But I just heard him say, my darling Annie,
as the moonlight revealed his hand on her . . .
goodnight, everybody, goodnight.

Gordon Miller
Portsmouth, Hampshire

*Tune: 'The Eton Boating Song'*

The sexual life of the camel
is not what everyone thinks.
One day at the height of its passion
it decided to bugger the Sphinx.
Now the Sphinx's sexual orifice
was blocked up by the sands of the Nile,
which explains the hump of the camel
and the Sphinx's inscrutable smile.

Lynne Thomson, 44
Chippenham, Wiltshire

The captain of the lugger,
he was a dirty bugger,
he wasn't fit to shovel shit
from one ship to another.

CHORUS
Frigging on the rigging
Frigging on the rigging
Frigging on the rigging
'cos there's nothing else to do
'cos there's nothing else to do.

His wife's name it was Mabel:
she thought that she was able
to castrate the first mate
on the galley table.

CHORUS . . .

Paul Davis
NSW, Australia

*Tune: 'I'm looking over the white cliffs of Dover'*

I'm looking under a skirt of wonder
that I've underlooked before.
First come the ankles,
then come the knees,
then come the knickers
which flap in the breeze.
No need explaining
the one remaining
that I just simply adore.
I'm looking under a skirt of wonder
that I've underlooked before.

Paul Davis
NSW, Australia

*Tune: 'All Creatures that on Earth Do Dwell'*

As I was passing Parliament
I stuck my foot in excrement.
I cried for help but no help came
and so I stuck my foot in it again.

As I was passing through a wood
I shat myself, I knew I would.
I cried for help but no help came
and so I shat myself again.

As I was passing by St Paul's
a lady grabbed me by the balls.
I cried for help but no help came.
and so she grabbed my balls again.

J. O. Bartlett
Portsmouth, Hampshire

*Tune: signature tune for 'Fraggle Rock'*

Down at Fraggle Rock
grab a Fraggle by its cock,
whirr it round your head
till that stupid Fraggle's dead.
If you're not sure,
slam its bollocks in the door.
Then you get a rock
and throw it at its cock,
down at Fraggle Rock.

Boy, 13
London


Now old Mother Riley
in London did dwell,
a dirty old woman
I knew her quite well.
She went to the doctor's
'cos she couldn't shite,
and he gave her some pills
saying, 'You'll be alright.'

Singing, brown, brown, dirty old brown.

Now old Mother Riley
she went home to bed,
she bounced on her tits,
and bounced on her head.
Now old Mother Riley
she was an old cuss,
and out of the window
she stuck her great ass.

Singing, brown, brown, dirty old brown.

Now Percy the Policeman
was out on the beat,
by very same chance
he was up that same street.
He looked to the stars
and he looked to the sky,
and a Mach 15 turd
hit him smack in the eye.

Singing, brown, brown, dirty old brown.

Now Percy the Policeman,
he cussed and he swore,
he called old Ma Riley
a dirty old whore.
He went round the village
that very same night,
with a note round his neck
saying, 'Blinded by shite!'

Singing, brown, brown, dirty old brown.

Ian Thomas, 47
Lydney, Gloucestershire

*Tune: signature tune for 'Scooby Doo'*

Scooby dooby doo,
where are you?
In the toilet,
doin' a poo.
How much have you done?
More than a ton.
If you don't shut up
I'll do it on you.

Boy, 11
London

*Tune: 'Teddy Bear's Picnic'*

If you go down in the woods today,
you'll surely have a surprise.
If you go down in the woods today,
you'll never believe your eyes.
'cos Mum and Dad are having a shag
and Uncle Bob is licking his knob
and Winnie the Pooh is having a screw
with Grandma.

Jodie, 14
Plymouth, Devon


## Teenage Mutant Hero Turtles

Down in the sewers
where nobody goes
there's one fat rat
picking his nose.
Along came Shredder
thin as a stick.
He thought he did karate
but he chopped off his dick.

Jodie, 14
Plymouth, Devon

We are the Whitleigh girls
we wear our hair in curls.
We wear our dungarees
up to our bums and knees.
We wear our daddies' shirts
we wear our mummies' skirts.
You know that boy next door?
He got me on the floor.
My mummy was surprised
to see my belly rise.
My daddy jumped for joy –
it was a baby boy.

Jodie, 14
Plymouth, Devon

There's a shortage of bog paper in Brazil
there's a shortage of bog paper in Brazil
there's a shortage of bog paper
so they wait until it's vapour
then they light it with a taper
in Brazil.

In Brazil, in Brazil
in Brazil, in Brazil
there's a shortage of bog paper
so they wait until it's vapour
then they light it with a taper
in Brazil.

There's a shortage of good whores in Brazil
there's a shortage of good whores in Brazil
there's a shortage of good whores
but there's keyholes in the doors
and there's knotholes in the floors
in Brazil.

In Brazil, in Brazil
in Brazil, in Brazil
there's a shortage of good whores
but there's keyholes in the doors
and there's knotholes in the floors
in Brazil.

There's a shortage of wine glasses in Brazil
there's a shortage of wine glasses in Brazil
there's a shortage of wine glasses
'cos the English upper classes
shove wine glasses up their arses
in Brazil.

In Brazil, in Brazil
in Brazil, in Brazil
there's a shortage of wine glasses
'cos the English upper classes
shove wine glasses up their arses
in Brazil.

There was a man called Hunt in Brazil
there was a man called Hunt in Brazil.
there was a man called Hunt
and he thought he had a cunt
but his arse was back to front
in Brazil.

In Brazil, in Brazil
in Brazil, in Brazil
there was a man called Hunt
and he thought he had a cunt
but his arse was back to front
in Brazil.

There was a man called Best in Brazil
there was a man called Best in Brazil
there was a man called Best
and he thought he had a breast
but his balls were on his chest
in Brazil.

In Brazil, in Brazil,
in Brazil, in Brazil
there was a man called Best
and he thought he had a breast
but his balls were on his chest
in Brazil.

Man, 31
Watford, Hertfordshire

*Tune: 'Postman Pat'*

Spaceman Pat
Spaceman Pat
Spaceman Pat and his black-and-white cat
flying over Venus
playing with his penis.
Isn't he a very naughty boy?

Everybody knows his penis glows.
All the girls scream as he passes by,
maybe your luck is in
he will stop.
Flash!
You'll never be the same.
Spaceman Pat
Spaceman Pat
Spaceman Pat and his black-and-white cat.

Steph, 17
Peterborough, Cambridgeshire

*Tune: 'My Old Man's a Dustman'*

My old Granny's a psycho
she blows up people's houses
she's got armour-plated false teeth
and got piranhas in her trousers.

Her letterbox is fitted
with a large machine gun,
and in the pub she breaks open nuts
with the straining of her bum.

Yes, my old Granny's a psycho
and her eyes they burn like fires.
She's got a Harley instead of a rocking-chair
and she's pierced her nipples with pliers.

My Granny's a raver
you'll probably see her one day
as my old psycho Granny
bombs it down the M1 motorway.

Khristina Rainford
Liverpool

*Tune: signature tune for 'Rainbow'*

Up above the streets and houses,
Bungle flying high,
Jeffrey sticks his dick out the window
and pokes Bungle in the eye.
Bungle takes a maddy
and he runs up all the stairs,
grabs ahold of Jeffrey's cock
and pulls out all the hairs.

Scott Divit, 14
Fife, Scotland


*Tune: 'Oh, I had the wings of an angel'*

Oh, I wish I had the balls of a donkey
and the prick of a prize kangaroo.
I would fuck all the girls in creation
and send my results to the zoo.

E. V. Ryley
Winburg, South Africa

*Tune: signature tune for 'Captain Pugwash'*

When your balls hang low,
let them dangle in the snow.
When you get a funny feeling,
you can whitewash any ceiling.
Let your mind go blank,
when you're gasping for a wank,
singing, 'Nelly, put your belly next to mine.'

Jim, 38
Wirral, Merseyside


*Tune: 'D'ye ken John Peel'*

D'ye ken John Peel
with his prick of steel,
his balls of brass
and a cardboard arse?
Well, he fucked all night
till his balls were tight
and he still had the horn in the morning.

Gordon Miller
Portsmouth, Hampshire

I was in the most famous regiment of Great Britain, the Skin Back Fusiliers, and our song was:

Left, right, skin back tight,
bollocks to the front
we are the boys
who make no noise
when we are chasing cunt.
We are the heroes of the night,
we would sooner fuck than fight,
we are the boys of the Skin Back Fusiliers.

Gordon Miller
Portsmouth, Hampshire

*Tune: 'Three Little Fishes'*

Ring-dang-do and what is that?
Black and furry like a cat.
Hole in the middle and a big one too,
that's what they call a Ring-dang-do.

My old Pop when he was young,
used to like to have his fun.
Ticklin' Ma with his big bamboo
and shovin' it up her Ring-dang-do.

Man, 62
Victoria, Australia

*Tune: 'Tit-willow, tit-willow'*

On a tree by a river a little tom-tit
sang, 'Willow tit-willow, tit-willow.'
And I said to him, 'Dicky-bird, why do you shit
on my head? Oh, willow, tit-willow.
Do you have bad diarrhoea?' I cried,
'or a vindaloo curry that's way down inside?'
With a burp and a fart and a groan he replied,
'Oh, willow tit-willow tit-willow.'

The bird let one rip as he sat on that bough
singing, 'Willow tit-willow tit-willow.'
Then he did a huge dump though I'm not sure how –
oh, willow tit-willow tit-willow.
I managed to dodge as it fell to the ground
with a whiff I should think spread for miles around,
and from way up above came a delicate sound
'Oh, willow tit-willow tit-willow . . .'

Lucy Day, 17
Enfield, Middlesex

*Tune: 'Good King Wenceslas'*

Good King Wenceslas looked out
o'er his fields of snow,
saw the bushes shaking about,
sighed and said, 'Oh no!

There they are again,' he said,
'those two furtive lovers.
I wouldn't mind so much,' he said,
'if they had duvet covers.'

Alistair Whyte, 13
Forfar, Scotland


*Tune: 'Colonel Bogey'*

Mummy, you know the boy next door?
Mummy, he got me on the floor.
Mummy, you see my tummy
getting bigger and bigger each day.

Herbert, what have you done to me?
Herbert, we'll start a family.
Herbert, we'll call him Sherbet
and there'll be Herbert, Sherbet and me.

Miss A. Grant, 10
Loughborough, Leicestershire

*Tune: 'Get down on it'*

Get down on it,
suck my bonnet,
please don't bite it,
just excite it.

Boy, 12
London

*Tune of chorus: 'Do wa diddy diddy dum diddy day'*

This is number one
and the story's just begun,
singing: Do what Daddy did to Mummy to make me.

This is number two
and he's taken off my shoe,
singing: Do what Daddy did to Mummy to make me.

This is number three
and he's undressing me,
singing: Do what Daddy did to Mummy to make me.

This is number four
and he's got me on the floor,
singing: Do what Daddy did to Mummy to make me.

This is number five
and he's doing a dirty dive,
singing: Do what Daddy did to Mummy to make me.

This is number six
and he's playing with my tits,
singing: Do what Daddy did to Mummy to make me.

This is number seven
and it feels like heaven,
singing: Do what Daddy did to Mummy to make me.

This is number eight
and the nurse is at the gate,
singing: Do what Daddy did to Mummy to make me.

This is number nine
and the twins are feeling fine,
Singing: Do what Daddy did to Mummy to make me.

This is number ten
and we're doing it all again,
Singing: Do what Daddy did to Mummy to make me.

Daniel Edwards, 12
London

*Tune: 'Hi-ho Hi-ho'*

Hi ho, hi ho,
it's off to work we go
with a walking stick
and a hairy dick
Hi ho, hi ho, hi ho, hi ho.

Claire, 10
Banbury, Oxfordshire

*Tune: 'My Grandfather's Clock'*

My grandfather's cock
was too large for himself,
so it dragged ninety years on the floor.
It was longer by half
than the old man himself
and it weighed half a hundredweight more.
It went on the horn
the moment he was born –
it was always his joy and pride.
But it stopped, shrank,
never to go again,
when the old . . . man . . . died.

Man, 52
Radcliffe-on-Trent, Nottingham

*Tune: 'El Paso'*

**El Crappo**

Out in the west Texas town of El Paso
I ate a very hot Mexican dish.
Night-time would find me in Rose's Cantina.
They said it was meat but it smelt just like fish.

At last here I am in the bog in the town of El Paso
I pay my money and make a loud din.
Five seconds later, I'm writhing in anguish.
It's as hot coming out as it was going in.

Dave Walden, 50
Lynton, North Devon

*Tune: 'My Favourite Things'*

Wankers and perverts
and whiskers on minges,
big tits and arseholes
and alcohol binges,
gold skid-marked underpants
tied up with string –
these are a few of my favourite things.

Dave Parker, 52
Aylesbury, Buckinghamshire

78

*Tune: 'Eton Boating Song'*

The sexual life of an ostrich
Is the greatest in all the land.
At the height of the mating season
It buries its head in the sand.
Now supposing another ostrich
Should see its arse stuck in the air,
does it suck it or pluck it or fuck it?
Or doesn't it fucking well care?

Man, 52
Bolton, Lancashire

When he was six
he did a silly trick:
he slid right down the banister
and paralysed his . . .

. . . eye dingle dangle
dingle dangle di,
the funniest little boy
that ever was alive.

When he was married
he married Missy Hunt
and all the lads down the pub
called him a silly . . .

. . . eye dingle dangle
dingle dangle di,
the funniest little boy
that ever was alive.

When he was buried
they stuffed him up with grass,
and what they couldn't get down his throat
they rammed right up his . . .

. . . eye dingle dangle
dingle dangle di,
the funniest little boy
that ever was alive.

The Bog Up North (female)
Newbury, Berks

*Tune: 'Colonel Bogey'*

Hitler has only got one ball.
The other is in the Albert Hall.
His mother,
the silly bugger,
cut it off when he was small.
She hung it up on a chestnut tree.
The wind blew it out to sea.
The fishes,
who ate off dishes,
had rollocks and bollocks for tea.

Boy, 11
London

There once was a gay caballero,
exceedingly gay caballero,
who called his Long Tom
Marta-Marta-Marta Merino.

He went to a low-down casino,
exceedingly low-down casino,
and with him he took
Marta-Marta-Marta Merino.

There he met a gay senorita,
exceedingly gay senorita,
and to her he showed his
Marta-Marta-Marta Merino.

She showed him her white crevissino,
exceedingly white crevissino,
and in it he put his
Marta-Marta-Marta Merino.

It gave him a bad cocksore-ino,
exceedingly bad cocksore-ino,
which blackened the end of
Marta-Marta-Marta Merino.

He went to the great Doctorino,
exceedingly great Doctorino,
who cut off the end of
Marta-Marta-Marta Merino.

Now he sits on the gay Riviera,
exceedingly gay Riviera,
and fiddles with the stump of
Marta-Marta-Marta Merino.

Man, 52
Radcliffe-on-Trent, Nottingham

# Nursery Crimes

Hickory dickory dock,
three mice ran up the clock.
The clock struck one
the others escaped with minor injuries.

Andrew Copper
Beckenham, Kent


Little Jack Horner sat in the corner,
eating red hot scollops.
One dropped down
and burnt his knee,
completely missing his bollocks.

Andrew Copper
Beckenham, Kent

## Second World War News

Jack and Jill went up the hill
to play at hanky-panky.
Jill came down
with half-a-crown.
It must have been a Yankee.

Olwyn Jones, 33
(Heard from mum)
Tenbury Wells, Worcestershire


Little Jack Horner stood in the corner,
snogging the girl who gave him his pie.
He glanced down below
and wailed, 'Oh no!'
His plum was caught in his fly.

Naomi from London
Accrington, Lancashire

Hickory dickory dock
the mouse ran up the clock.
At half past three
he did a pee
and the small hand caught in his cock.

Naomi from London
Accrington, Lancashire


Hey diddle diddle
the cat did a fiddle,
the cow shit over the moon.
The little dog laughed to see such filth
and got hit in the balls by the spoon.

Tony George, 43
Stourbridge, West Midlands

Mary had a little dress,
the skirt was split in half,
and every step that Mary took
the boys could see her calf.
Mary had another dress
split high up in front,
but she never wore that one.

Claire Wilcock, 18
Nelson, Lancashire

Hey diddle diddle,
the poo and the piddle,
the yelling from midnight till noon.
The baby threw up all the day
and mother has gone to the moon.

Diarmid, Fergus, Roderick, 7
Edinburgh

Mary, Mary, quite contrary,
had a garden of grass.
While skipping along in the morning dew
she slipped and fell on her arse.

Girl, 12
London


Little Miss Muffet
sat on her tuffet
fingering herself away.
Along came a spider
sat down beside her
and said, 'Can I go all the way?'

J. Dent, 21
Norwich, Norfolk

The cat had a fiddle
with the cow that jumped over the moon.
The dog was so happy
he sat in his nappy
and had a fiddle with his own.

J. Dent, 21
Norwich, Norfolk


Mary had a little lamb,
its feet as black as charcoal.
Every time it jumped the fence
you saw its dirty arsehole.

S/SGT Adams, 37
Engineers

One, two
there's shit on my shoe.
Three, four,
there's a whore at the door.
Five six,
she wants my dick.
Nine, ten,
late for work again.
Eleven, twelve,
work it out for yourselves.

Naomi from London
Accrington, Lancashire

Mary had a little lamb
who used to scratch and fidget,
so she took it to the circus
so's she could fuck the midget.

Mary had a little lamb
she thought it diabolic,
she gave it brandy twice a day
and now it's alcoholic.

Nicola Colohan, 18
County Sligo, Eire

Mary had a little lamb,
she called him Orinoco,
she put him on the window-sill
and he peed in Granny's cocoa.

Sarah Pett-Noble, 23
Manchester


Rock-a-bye baby on the tree top
when the wind blows, the cradle will rock.
I was that baby and what bothers me
is why Mum and Dad shoved me up a tree.

Nicola Colohan, 18
County Sligo, Eire

The Grand Old Duke of York,
he had ten thousand men,
he took them all on top of the hill
and never came down again.

Sally Prager, 53
Luton, Bedfordshire

Little Jack Horner sat in a corner
feeling as randy as hell.
He took out his dick
and stuck it up quick
and surprised and shocked Little Nell.

Sally Jager, 53
Luton, Bedfordshire


Little Miss Muffet sat on a tuffet
her legs spread, inviting, apart.
Along came a spider
who strayed deep inside her
and was crushed to death in a fart.

Sally Jager, 53
Luton, Bedfordshire

Incey Wincey spider
climbed the water spout,
down came the rain
and washed poor Incey out.

Out came the sun
and dried up all the rain,
but Incey Wincey spider
had buggered off to Spain.

Emma, 18
Hainault, Middlesex

# A Dirty Little Poem from Limerick

There was an old man from Calcutta
Who was having a wank in the gutter.
A woman walked by,
got spunk in her eye,
and thought it was Ireland's best butter.

Andrew Copper
Beckenham, Kent

An over-sexed lady named Bright
insists on two dozen a night.
A fellow named Cheddar
had the brashness to wed 'er.
His chance of survival is slight.

Lynne Thomson, 44
Chippenham, Wiltshire


There was a young lady of West Ham
who went for a ride in a tram.
She kissed the conductor
who turned round and fucked her
and now she's pushing a pram.

Lynne Thomson, 44
Chippenham, Wiltshire

There once was a woman called Kit
who had a really big tit.
The boys used to stare
but she took great care
to find a bra that would fit.

Laura Benson, 12
Overall, Suffolk

There was a young man from Goole
who had a large strangely shaped tool.
If he chalked up the end
he'd play shots that would bend
and in this way he'd win games of pool.

David Thomsett-Palmer
Southport, Merseyside


There was a young lady called Pilling
who went to her dentist for filling.
Because of her depravity
he filled the wrong cavity,
now Pilling is nursing her filling.

Man, 58
Berkshire

There was a young girl from Cape Cod
who thought that all babies came from God.
But it wasn't the Almighty
who lifted her nightie
but Roger the Lodger, the sod.

Paul Davis
NSW, Australia


A vice most obscene and unsavoury
keeps the Bishop of Boston in slavery.
With lecherous howls,
he deflowers young owls
which he keeps in an underground aviary.

Dora Darling, 70
British Columbia, Canada


When Titian was mixing rose madder
his model climbed up a ladder.
Her position, to Titian,
suggested coition,
so he leapt up the ladder and had 'er.

Dora Darling, 70
British Columbia, Canada

There was once a young nun called Vera
who wouldn't let anyone near her,
when a crafty old monk
jumped into her bunk
and now she is a Mother Superior.

Jean, 70
County Down, Northern Ireland

There was a young woman called Jude
who went for a swim in the nude,
when a man in a punt
stuck his pole where he shouldn't
and said, 'You can't swim in here, love, it's private.'

Alexandra McCole, 24
Rochdale, Lancashire


There was a young man of Devizes
who had knackers of unequal sizes.
One was so small
it was no use at all,
but the other big bugger won prizes.

Jean, 70
County Down, Northern Ireland

There was once a young man from Harrow
who had a cock as big as a marrow.
He said to his tart,
'Hold this for a start,
'cos my balls are outside on the barrow.'

Sandra Musselwhite
London

There was an young man called Perkin
who couldn't stop jerkin' his gherkin.
His mother said, 'Perkin,
stop jerkin' your gherkin,
your gherkin's for ferkin', not jerkin'.'

Alexandra McCole, 24
Rochdale, Lancashire


A naughty young fellow called James
got up to some terrible games.
He set fire to the rim
of his old granny's quim
and laughed when she pissed on the flames.

Told by girl of 14
over fifty years ago to
John Bruce, 70
London

There was a man from Monata,
he was a champion farter.
He could fart anything
from 'God Save the King'
to Beethoven's 'Moonlight Sonata'.

E. V. Ryley
Winburg, South Africa

The Prior of Dunstan St Just,
consumed with erotical lust,
screwed the Bishop's prize fowls,
then five startled owls
and a little green lizard that bust.

R. Hoddinott
Chester


There was once a frivolous friar
who had an infernal desire.
The cause of his fall,
was not women at all.
It was a little boy out of the choir.

Mrs. F. Longson, 88
Buxton, Derbyshire

There was once a tar who got drunk
and fell asleep in his bunk.
He dreamt that Venus
tickled his penis
then floated away in the spunk.

Mrs F. Longson, 88
Buxton, Derbyshire

There was a young man from Water Orton –
by God, his dick was a very short'un.
To make up for the loss,
he had ears like a hoss
and a fart like a 600 Norton.

David G. Morris
Birmingham

There was a young man from St Paul's
who did a good turn on the halls.
His favourite trick
was to spin on his prick
and roll off the stage on his balls.

Margaret Jennings, 40
Lincoln

An ambitious young Aberdeen laddy
said he'd teach girls to golf and to caddy.
He accomplished these goals
in a fast eighteen holes
seventeen of which made him a daddy.

Claire Wilcock, 18
Nelson, Lancashire

There was a young girl from Hitchin
whose cunt was constantly itching.
Her mother said, 'Rose,
pox, I suppose?'
She said, 'Bollocks! Get on with your knitting.'

Margaret Jennings, 40
Lincoln

There was a young lady from Bude
who went for a swim in the lake.
A man in a punt
stuck an oar up her nose
and said, 'You can't swim in here, it's dangerous.'

Caroline, 16
Rutland

There was a surveyor from Ryde
who fell down a cesspool and died.
His brother from Tring
did the very same thing
and now they're interred side by side.

Architect, 65
Newbury, Berkshire

There was a young man named Cunningham
who stood on a bridge at Buckingham
watching the stunts
of the cunts in the punts
and the tricks of the pricks who were fucking 'em.

Man, 60s
Berkshire

There was a young maid of Ostend
who thought she'd hold out to the end.
But half way over
from Calais to Dover
she did what she didn't intend.

Sarah Mason
Clwyd, Wales

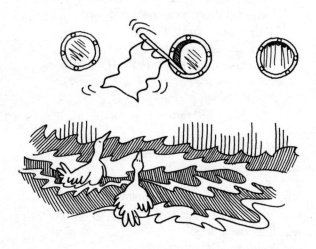

There was an old man from Darjeeling
who travelled from London to Ealing.
It said on the door,
'Please don't piss on the floor.'
So he carefully pissed on the ceiling.

Sarah Mason
Clwyd, Wales

Mary and Billy went for a romp
During foreplay Mary's mouth went chomp.
Billy discovered
his willy was buggered
and now he was left with a stump.

Andy Hayes, 15
Amersham, Buckinghamshire

There was a young man from Australia
who painted his arse like a dahlia.
The artwork was fine,
the painting divine,
but the smell was a bit of a failure.

Simon Tilbury, 15
Harrow, Middlesex

### Notice in train

*Sung to Dvořák's 'Humoresque'*

Passengers will please refrain
from making water on the train
while standing at the platform for a while.
We encourage constipation
till you reach your destination,
so sit back and bear it with a smile.

Mike Beal, 69
Plymouth, Devon


A bald man is a dick with ears.

The height of hunger is teeth marks on the toilet
    bowl.
The height of desperation is skid marks on the toilet
    seat.

Garett Murphy, 19
Pretoria, South Africa

### Advice to Snow White in winter

Beware of frigid midgets with rigid digits.

Paul Davis
NSW, Australia

A fart is the agonized scream of a trapped turd.

Paul Davis
NSW, Australia

Why is sex so noisy? Does it have to be so loud?
All that bloody moaning, well, it might attract a
  crowd.
'Cos when you're really at it, what on earth is there to
  gain,
By making such a racket, like you're in a lot of pain?
It starts off with the foreplay, and a breathless 'You're
  so good.'
Then comes, 'Oh, baby take me', till that deep
  orgasmic flood.

Ooohs and aaahs are everywhere, with screams of wild
  delight,
The headboard starts to rattle when you're bonking
  through the night.
But quiet sex is possible with skill, finesse and poise.
So basically the message is: Make Less Fucking
  Noise.

Jenny Wallace, 16
Scotland

The Conservative Party have chosen the condom as its official emblem, the reason being that it stands for inflation, halts production, gives protection to a bunch of pricks and gives one a false sense of security while being stuffed.

Lynne Thomson, 44
Chippenham, Wiltshire

No matter how you shake your peg,
the last wee drop runs down your leg.

Alix Lee, 21
Berkhamsted, Herts

Why work at an Esso Garage when . . .
. . . Esso means eat, sleep, shit and overtime.

Gordon Miller
Portsmouth, Hampshire

What's green and swings from trees?
Gorilla snot.

What's oral sex?
The taste of things to come.

What do you give an elephant that's got the shits?
Plenty of room.

Why are pubic hairs curly?
So they don't stick up your nose.

David G. Morris
Birmingham


Why do Tampax have strings?
So the crabs can bungee jump.

Khristina Rainford
Liverpool

What's the difference between a Durex and a coffin?
You come in one and go in the other.

What have a Durex and a coffin got in common?
They both hold stiffs.

What's the difference between oral sex and driving in
the fog?
With oral sex you can see the prick in front of you.

What is organic dental floss?
Pubic hair.

Why are men like nappies?
'Cos they hang around your arse all day and they're
usually full of shit.

What does the ideal lover (for women) look like?
Who cares, as long as he has a dick like a baby's arm
holding an orange
a twelve-inch tongue and can breathe through his ears.

What's the quickest way of putting the light on after
sex?
Open the car door.

Julie Cotter, 24
Mountain Ash, South Wales

## Say three times quickly

Old Granny Grunt
had a cuddy punt.
Not a cuddy punt
but a hunt punt cuddy.

Jodie, 14
Plymouth, Devon.

Agony is Cinderella's Tampax turning into a
    pumpkin.

Claire, 16
Rutland


There were seven dwarfs in the bath feeling happy . . .
. . . so Happy got out.

Caroline, 16
Rutland


'It looks nice out . . .'
. . . so he left it out all day.

Man, 47
London

What's the difference between a barrow-boy and a little sausage-dog?
One bawls out his wares and the other wears out his balls.

Man, 47
London

What are the three worst things about being an egg?

1. You only get laid once.
2. It takes you eight minutes to get hard.
3. The only person to sit on your face is your mother.

Anna Way, 19
Enfield, Middlesex

## Book

*The Brothers Hunt* (being the story of Joe, Mike and York) by John Thomas.

Paul Davis
NSW, Australia

## Notice

For parking so close, next time leave a fucking can
  opener so I can get my car out.

Jude, 21
Middlesex

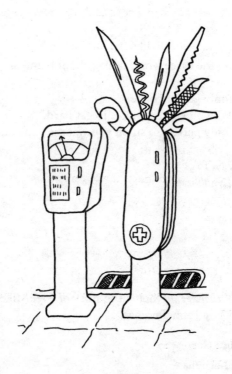

Join the Hernia Society. They need your support.

Lorraine Whyte, 22
County Antrim, Northern Ireland

Don't make love in a cornfield. Corn has ears.

Is love in a cornfield porn on the cob?

Lorraine Whyte, 22
County Antrim, Northern Ireland

Man has seventeen parts that won't work:

10 nails that won't work
2 calves that won't calf
2 tits that won't milk
2 balls that won't bounce
1 cock that won't crow . . .

. . . but women have got a pussy that won't catch
mice.

Angelina Curzey, 17
Birmingham

A young boy was walking across the common and he saw a man and a woman making love, so he ran off and got a policeman.

The next day when they were in court, the judge said to the little boy, 'Now son, tell the court in your own words, what the couple were doing.'

So the little boy said, 'They was fucking, sir.'

And the judge said, 'Go and wash your mouth out and when you come back tell the court again.'

So the little boy came back and repeated what he had said first, 'They was fucking, sir.'

This went on for about six times and the judge got so fed up he said, 'Now son, in your OWN words, what were they doing?'

So the little boy said,

> 'Well, sir, her blouse was torn
> her tits were bare
> his knob was swaying in the air.
> He shoved it in, she gave a grunt
> if that's not fucking, I'm a . . .'

Sandra Musselwhite
London

What do you call a rabbit with a bent dick?
Fucks Funny

What's the last thing that goes through a bug's mind
   before hitting the windshield at 80 mph?
Its arsehole.

Andrew Williamson, 19
Warley, West Midlands

### Problem

If boys have foreskins,
how many do girls have?

Reg, 65
Newbury, Berkshire

It's long and thin,
covered with skin,
goodness knows how many
holes it's been in.

What is it?
A worm.

Dave Harrison, 57
Saltash, Cornwall

What's stiff and excites women?
Elvis Presley.

What's the difference between broccoli and snot?
Kids hate the taste of broccoli.

Why do ballerinas wear tights?
So when they do the splits they don't stick to the
    floor.

How do you screw a fat lady?
Roll her in flour and go for the wet spots.

Lyn Shapland
Queensland, Australia

Indecison: you're up to your neck in a bathful of shit
   and someone throws another bucket of it at you. Do
   you duck?

Vicky Arnold, 14
Barnstaple, Devon



It's hard to be good.
It has to be hard to be good.

Girl, 14
London



What's the difference between hard and light?
You can sleep with a light on.

Adrien J. Dyson, 25
Haywards Heath, West Sussex

Agony is a man with one arm and an itchy dick
    hanging from a cliff.
Stupidity is scratching it.

Innocence is nuns working in a condom factory,
    thinking they are making sleeping bags for worms.

Girl, 14
Hatfield, Herts.

What is the difference between someone in the
    Salvation Army and a girl in the bath?
One has a soul full of hope and the other has a hole
    full of soap.

What is the difference between a Trafalgar Square
    pigeon and a mountain goat?
One mucks around in the fountain, the other fucks
    around the mountain.

Do infants in infancy have less fun than adults in
    adultery?

Mike Beal, 69
Plymouth, Devon

I don't drink and I don't smoke and I only swear
  when it slips out.

Told by girl of 13
over fifty years ago to
John Bruce, 70
London

# A Total Walls-up

**Written on toilet walls, University of Pretoria, South Africa**

Here I sit and contemplate.
Should I shit or masturbate?

There's nothing wrong with sex on television, so long
  as you don't fall off.

Physicists phuck phrogs:
Chemists are chunts.

Save the trees, kill a woodpecker.

Keep the world green; fuck a frog.

Snip-snap and Bob's your auntie.

Some came here to sit and think,
Some came here to shit and stink,
Some came here to scratch their balls,
I came here to read the walls.

Garett Murphy, 19
Pretoria, South Africa

## Written on a toilet wall

Life is like a pubic hair on a toilet seat.
Some days you can get pissed off.

Angelina Curzey, 17
Birmingham

### Written on the toilet wall of a factory

My wife has two cunts.
I'm one of them for working here.

Dave Harrison, 57
Saltash, Cornwall

### Written on a toilet wall

*A message below a six-inch nail sticking out of the wall:*

Should you get stuck for paper,
use this nail as an arse-hole scraper.

*Elsewhere, same toilet*

I laugh with glee
I jump for joy
for I was here
before Kilroy.

Wipe that smile
off your face.
Kilroy built
the bloody place.

Tony George, 43
Stourbridge, West Midlands

## Written on a toilet wall

Here I sit, bloody bored,
playing with my tampon cord.

Karen Ricketts, 23
Southampton, Hampshire


## Written on a toilet wall

'Spider, spider, on the wall,
Have you any balls at all?,

' 'Course I have, you silly cunt,
You're looking at me back to front.'

Alexandra McCole, 24
Rochdale, Lancashire

## Written on a toilet wall

Shit-house writers when they die
will find erected in the sky
a monument dedicated to their wit:
a massive mountain of solid . . .

Paul Davis
NSW, Australia

## Written on a toilet wall

Judging from this show of wit,
Shakespeare's ghost came here to shit.

E. V. Ryley
Winburg, South Africa

## Written above the urinal

Stand closer. It's shorter than you think.

Paul Davis
NSW, Australia

*Published or forthcoming*

# CAUTION! USED CARS

**Philip D. Turner**

*Caution! Used Cars* is packed with expert, up-to-the-minute information to help you buy a better used car and sell the one you own. You can find out how to:

Ensure a car is roadworthy before you buy it

Learn your rights as a consumer

Guard against buying a stolen or clocked car

and much, much more.

'Straightforward, honest and useful … Full of sensible advice on when, how and what to purchase' – *Daily Telegraph*